Microlife
That Helps Us

Steve Parker

Raintree

Chicago, Illinois

For information, address the publisher:
Raintree, 100 N. LaSalle, Suite 1200
Chicago, IL 60602
Customer Service 888-363-4266
Visit our website at www.raintreelibrary.com

Printed and bound in China by South China Printing Company Ltd
10 09 08 07 06
10 9 8 7 6 5 4 3 2 1

Edited by Katie Orchard
Designed by Tim Mayer
Picture Research by Lynda Lines and Frances Bailey
Production by Duncan Gilbert

Library of Congress Cataloging-in-Publication Data
Parker, Steve.
  Microlife that helps us / Steve Parker
     p. cm. -- (The amazing world of microlife)
  Includes bibliographical references and index.
  ISBN 1-4109-1845-9 (lib. bdg. : hardcover) --
  ISBN 1-4109-1850-5 (pbk.)
1. Microbial ecology--Juvenile literature. 2. Host-parasite relationships--Juvenile literature   I. Title.
II. Series: Parker, Steve. Amazing world of microlife

QR100.P37 2005
579'.163--dc22

2005004229

Acknowledgments
The publishers would like to thank the following for permission to reproduce photographs: Corbis p. **11** (Stephen Welstead/LWA); Getty Images pp. **15** (Brook Slezak/Stone), **16** (3D Clinic), **24** (Josh Mitchell/Stone); photolibrary.com pp. **3** (James H. Robinson), **26** (Bob Stefko), **29** (James H. Robinson); Science Photo Library pp. **1** (VVG), **4** (David Scharf), **5** (J. C. Revy), **6** (CNRI), **8** (David Scharf), **9** (Adrienne Hart-Davis), **10** (Andrew Syred), **13** (Mark Clarke), **14** (Dr. Gopal Murti), **17** (VVG), **18** (M. Dauenheimer/Custom Medical Stock), **19** (Bouhier/BSIP Laurent), **20** (Ian Boddy), **21** (Maximilian Stock Ltd.), **23** (A. B. Dowsett/CAMR), **25** (Andrew Syred), **27** (David Scharf), **28** (VVG); Still Pictures p. **12** (Hartmut Schwarzbach); Topfoto p. **22** (Timothy Ross/The Image Works); Tudor Photography p. **7**.

Contents

Some words are shown in bold, **like this**. You can find out what they mean by looking in the Glossary.

Our Tiny Helpers

We are surrounded by helpers. They make our lives better. Some helpers are our family and friends, who take care of us and do things for us. Some helpers are minibeasts—small creatures such as bees and spiders. And some helpers are microlife—tiny creatures and other living things that are too small to see.

Some of our microhelpers are bugs called **bacteria**, shown here 5,000 times larger than real life.

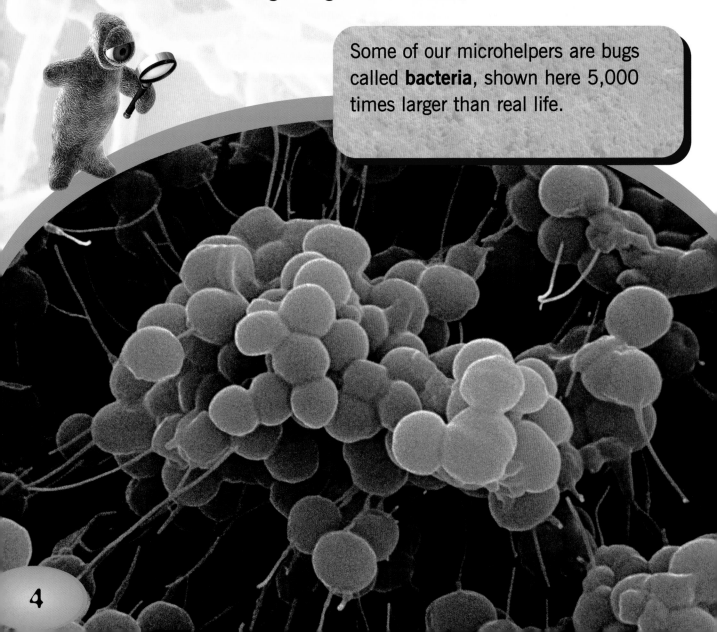

A microscope shows tiny grains of **pollen** on a bee's legs (seen here as tiny white dots). The bee gathers pollen from flowers and uses it to make honey.

pollen grains

Mini and micro

We can easily see our minibeast helpers. Bees make tasty honey, which we like to eat. Spiders eat pests such as flies. But our microhelpers can be thousands of times smaller—much too small to see with our eyes. We need a magnifying glass, or even a **microscope**, to make them look bigger. Then we can see them clearly.

Keeping Clean

Some of the smallest living things are **bacteria**. About 1,000 bacteria would fit on to the period at the end of this sentence. Bacteria live almost everywhere—in air, water, soil, and even inside our own bodies. Some bacteria are harmful. We call the harmful bacteria "germs." But other bacteria are helpful, or friendly, in many ways.

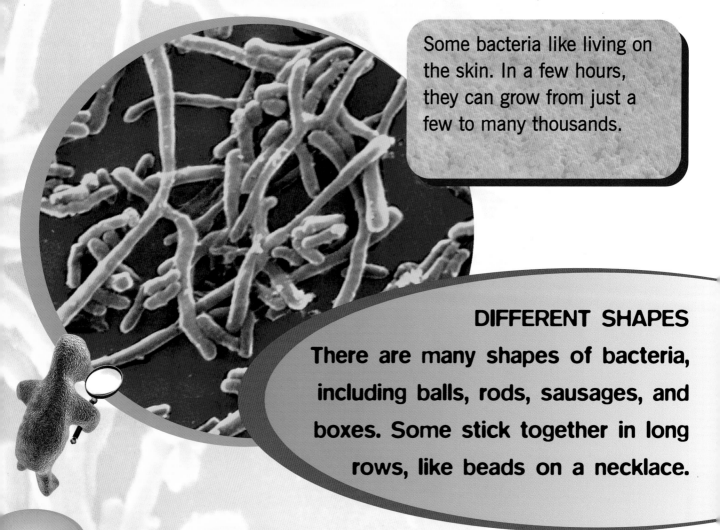

Some bacteria like living on the skin. In a few hours, they can grow from just a few to many thousands.

DIFFERENT SHAPES
There are many shapes of bacteria, including balls, rods, sausages, and boxes. Some stick together in long rows, like beads on a necklace.

Good and bad

Bacteria are always floating in the air and landing on us. Some friendly bacteria feed on the tiny flakes of our dead skin. They leave behind substances that other, harmful bacteria do not like. So helpful bacteria keep the harmful bacteria away. However, we must wash our skin often. Too many bacteria can collect on the skin and cause pimples, sores, and other problems.

We should always wash our hands before touching food or eating. This helps get rid of harmful bacteria and other microlife.

Microbakers

Do you have a favorite sandwich? Or do you like a toasted bagel? These foods are made with bread—and bread is made by helpful microlife. The tiny living things that do this are called **yeasts**. Hundreds of yeasts would fit into this "o."

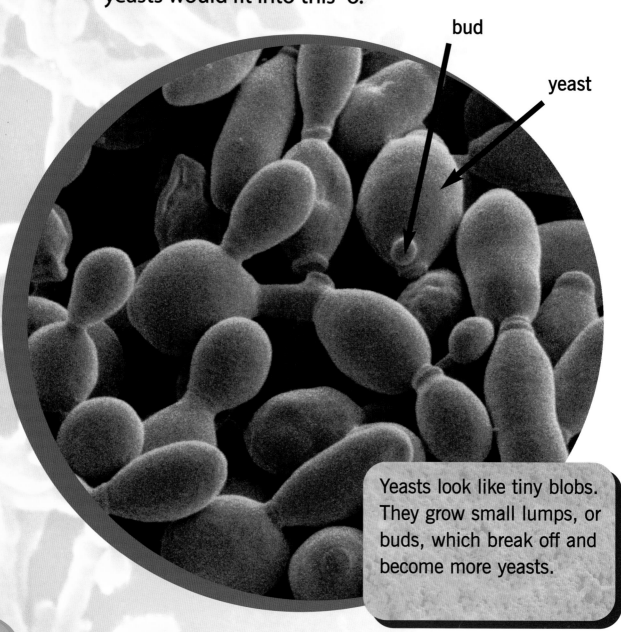

bud

yeast

Yeasts look like tiny blobs. They grow small lumps, or buds, which break off and become more yeasts.

Warm and bubbly

Yeasts are types of living things known as **fungi**. We make bread using baker's yeasts. They are mixed with a lump of dough, which is made from flour. The dough is baked in the oven. As the yeasts get warm, they make tiny bubbles. The bubbles collect to form small holes in the bread. The holes make the bread grow bigger and softer. We say that the bread "rises" as it bakes.

Look at this bread. You can see the small holes or bubbles made by millions of yeasts.

SPECIAL CHEESE

Some people do not eat any foods that come from animals. Most cheese is made from animal milk. But **vegetarian** cheese contains nothing from animals. It is made using a type of yeast called *lactis*.

Tasty Mold

When old food goes bad, or **moldy**, we throw it away. Moldy food can make us sick. But some kinds of molds are very tasty! They give flavor and color to certain foods. These special molds are grown in the food in a very careful way, so they are safe to eat.

The dark mold on blue cheese is called *Penicillium*. Another kind of *Penicillium* makes a germkilling medicine called **penicillin** (see page 21).

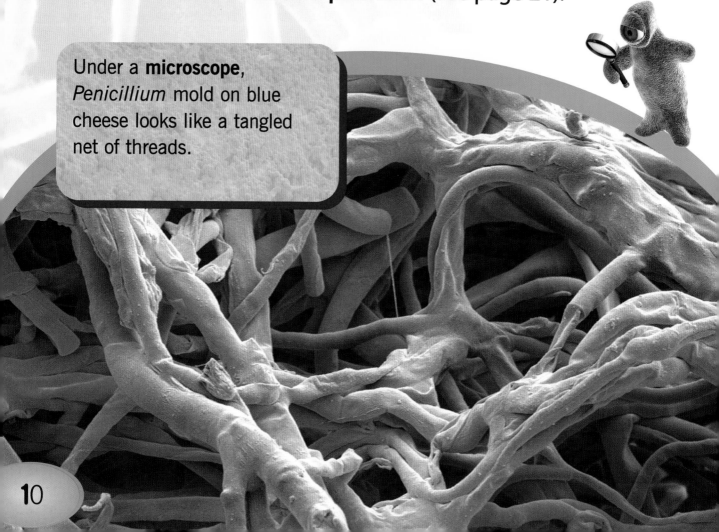

Under a **microscope**, *Penicillium* mold on blue cheese looks like a tangled net of threads.

We eat foods like bread and cheese when they are fresh. Otherwise, microfungi will turn them moldy.

Cheese and sauce

Molds are living things called **fungi** (like **yeasts**). The cheese called blue Stilton has patches of special dark mold running through it. Another cheese, Camembert, has white mold. Another type of tasty mold is called *Aspergillus*, which is used to make soy sauce. *Aspergillus* is also used to make citric acid, which helps to flavor foods and make them keep longer.

Clean, Safe Water

When we turn on a faucet, we get pure, clear, clean water. It is safe to use for drinking, cooking, and washing. Our tap water is made with the help of microlife. This microlife is found at the waterworks or water treatment centers, where our water is made safe.

DANGEROUS WATER
Not everyone in the world has clean, safe water. Millions of people drink untreated water from ponds, rivers, lakes, and ditches. This water often carries germs and disease.

Water is checked at the water treatment center to make sure it is pure. It is then sent along pipes to our homes.

Our bodies need plenty of clean, safe water every day to stay healthy.

Cleaning water

First, the water is taken from a river, lake, or well. At the treatment center, it trickles through many layers of small stones and sand. These remove, or filter, bits and pieces of dirt. Then the water is filtered through more layers, where billions of special **bacteria** live. These helpful bacteria eat, or destroy, harmful substances.

Microfizz

If you take a big gulp of a carbonated drink, the bubbles may go up your nose! Carbonated drinks such as ginger beer and root beer are made from water and sugar. They get their flavor from plant roots, berries, and spices. Then microlife is added— tiny, blob-shaped **fungi** called **yeasts**.

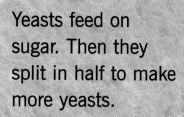

Yeasts feed on sugar. Then they split in half to make more yeasts.

TOO MUCH FIZZ

Making your own carbonated drinks with yeasts can be dangerous. If there is too much yeast, too many bubbles are made. These may press so hard on the bottle that it bursts with a huge BANG!

Making bubbles

As the drink is made, the yeasts feed on the sugar. They produce tiny bubbles. Then the drink is put into bottles with tight tops or stoppers. Inside, the bubbles stay very small. When the top is taken off the bottle, the bubbles can get bigger. This is what makes the carbonation.

If we gulp down a carbonated drink too fast, the bubbles come back up and make us burp.

Our Hidden Helpers

Some microlife helps us in a way that we cannot see—because it is inside us. Helpful microlife called **bacteria** live naturally in the body, mainly in our intestines (guts). There are billions of bacteria there, of more than 100 different kinds. Altogether, the bacteria in your guts would fill three coffee cups.

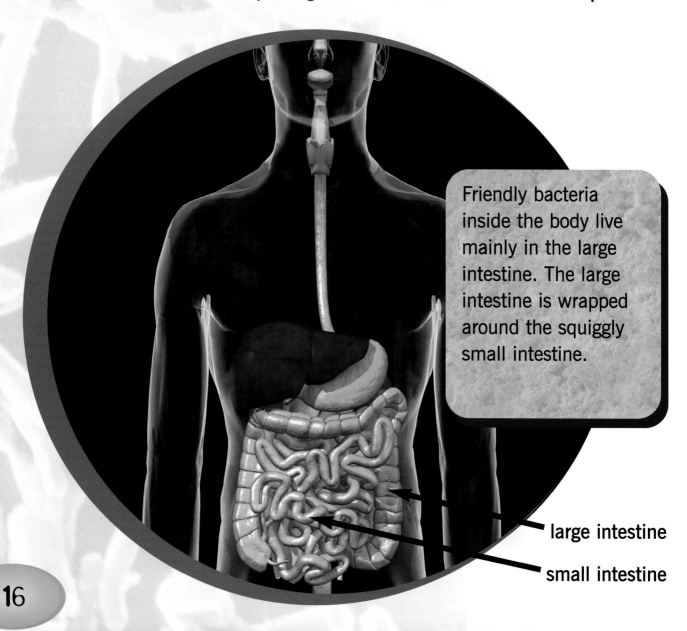

Friendly bacteria inside the body live mainly in the large intestine. The large intestine is wrapped around the squiggly small intestine.

large intestine

small intestine

We give the friendly *E. coli* bacteria inside us warmth and food. In exchange, they help us to take in the nutrients from our meals.

How bacteria help

Every day, these friendly bacteria help to break apart, or digest, our food. Then we can get more **nutrients** from it. Some friendly bacteria also make important substances called vitamins. Our bodies need vitamins to stay healthy and keep away disease.

HELP AND HARM
The friendly bacteria inside us include some kinds of *E. coli*. But other kinds of *E. coli* can cause problems such as stomachaches and food poisoning.

Staying Healthy

Some **bacteria** float in the air. They are so small that we cannot see them. As we breathe in and out, some of these bacteria get into the nose, mouth, throat, and chest. We breathe in a mixture of good and bad bacteria. Some good bacteria help us by stopping the bad ones from increasing in numbers and causing illness.

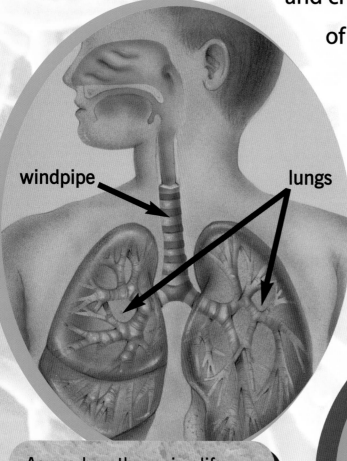

windpipe

lungs

As we breathe, microlife floats into the body's air passages—the nose, mouth, throat, windpipe, and lungs.

STREP THROAT
There are several kinds of bacteria called *Streptococcus*. Some are helpful. Some have little effect on us. But some cause the soreness called Strep throat.

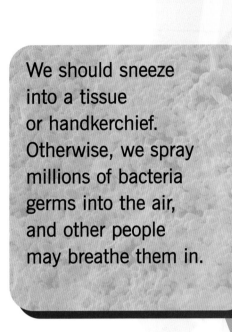

We should sneeze into a tissue or handkerchief. Otherwise, we spray millions of bacteria germs into the air, and other people may breathe them in.

Causing illness

The body must be healthy for the good bacteria to help us. We need to eat healthy foods, get plenty of exercise, and get enough sleep. If we do not take care of ourselves, the good bacteria cannot control the bad ones—and then the bad bacteria can take over. They may cause illnesses such as colds, coughs, and sore throats.

Making Medicine

When people are sick, they may need medicine. Some medicine is made by certain kinds of **bacteria** and **fungi**. It is grown in watery liquid, which bubbles and froths in a large tank. The microlife feeds in the liquid and is kept warm. Now and then, some of the liquid is taken from the tank, and the pure medicine is made from it.

GROWING PROPERLY
Some babies and children do not grow as fast as others. A medicine made by *E. coli* bacteria helps them to catch up and grow normally.

Much of the medicine we take is made by microlife.

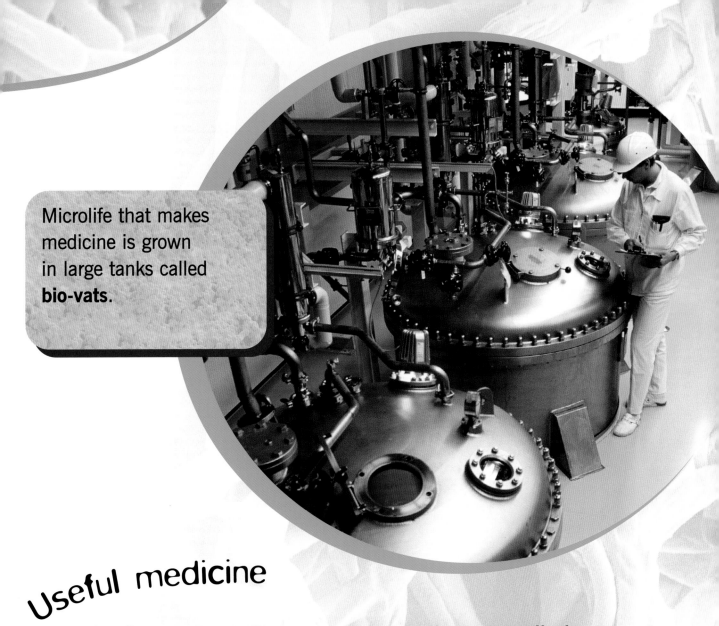

Microlife that makes medicine is grown in large tanks called **bio-vats**.

Useful medicine

The fungus *Penicillium* produces a substance called **penicillin**. Penicillin is used to make a medicine called an **antibiotic**, which kills harmful bacteria.

The bacteria *E. coli* can be changed so that they make a medicine called insulin. This is needed by some people who have an illness called **diabetes**. Without insulin, people who have diabetes may become very sick.

Preventing Disease

Have you had any "shots," or **injections**, to prevent you from catching certain diseases? These injections put substances called **vaccines** into the body. Different vaccines protect the body against diseases such as measles, mumps, and whooping cough.

BOOSTERS

Most "shots" or injections are given when we are young. To protect against some diseases, we may need an extra injection or "booster" when we are grown-up.

An injection may sting slightly, for just a few seconds—but it protects the body against serious illness for years and years.

What vaccines do

Some vaccines contain a small amount of the germs that cause a disease. These germs have been killed or changed so they cannot grow in the body and start the disease. When the vaccine is given, the body learns how to recognize and fight these germs. If the real germs get into the body later, the body can kill them all quickly, before the disease begins.

The germs in this vaccine have been killed so that they cannot cause an illness.

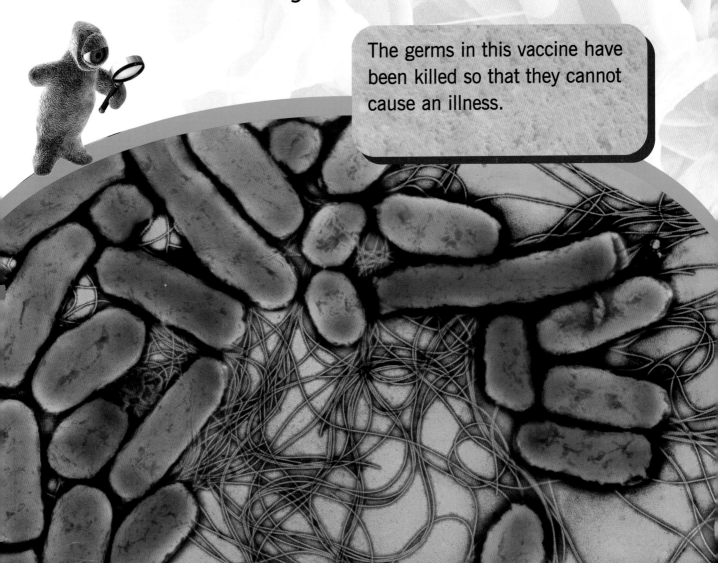

Back to Health

Some foods and drinks help us to get better after we have been sick. Some keep the inside of the body working well. They include special kinds of milk and yogurt. They are called health foods or health drinks—and they contain microlife.

Some people have health food and drinks every day. Others use them now and again, to help recover from illness.

Yogurt drinks

Yogurt is made from milk by adding the microlife called *Lactobacillus*. This name means "milk **bacteria**." As the *Lactobacillus* grows, the milk becomes thicker and slightly sour. This gives the yogurt its special taste. The microlife in the yogurt helps the body to get more nutrients from food. It may also stop some harmful germs from growing.

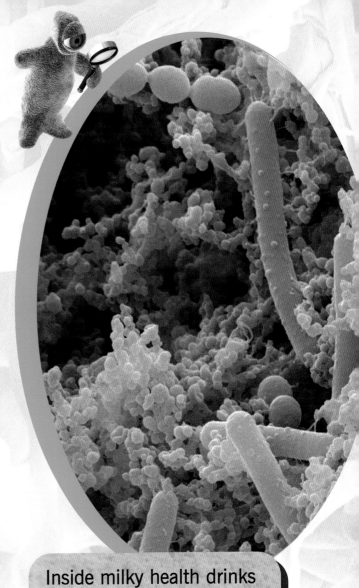

Inside milky health drinks are millions of bacteria that are good for the body.

LOTS OF HELPERS

In health drinks like special milks and yogurts, one drop the size of this "o" contains more than 10,000 helpful bacteria.

Microgardeners

Many kinds of microlife and minibeasts give help to plants and trees. Some help flowers to make their seeds and fruits. Flowers make tiny pieces of yellow dust, called **pollen** grains. For a flower to make its seeds or fruits, it must receive pollen grains from another flower of its kind. Some flowers need the help of certain minibeasts to do this.

As wasps and other creatures visit flowers, they spread pollen grains from other flowers.

SWEET HONEY

Bees take pollen and nectar back to their homes. There they make the nectar into a thick liquid, which is their food store. We take this liquid and eat it ourselves—it is called honey.

Pollen grains are very tiny. Many have spikes or hooks, which catch onto the legs and bodies of minibeasts.

Nectar and pollen

Many flowers make a sweet liquid called **nectar**. All kinds of minibeasts, such as beetles, moths, butterflies, bees, and ants, drink this nectar. As they drink, pollen grains stick to them. Then the minibeasts visit other flowers, to drink more nectar. The pollen they carry with them rubs off on these other flowers.

Beating the Pests

Some microlife and minibeasts are killers. This can be lucky for us, because they kill and eat other harmful living things. The helpful pest-eaters include many kinds of beetles, bugs, and spiders. Some of these are so small we can hardly see them.

A baby spider is almost as small as the dot of this "i." But already it is a fierce hunter.

Ladybugs and spiders

Tiny bugs called aphids, or greenflies, suck juices from plants. They can ruin a gardener's fruit bushes, roses, and other flowers. The brightly colored beetles called ladybugs love to eat aphids, so they are very helpful. Some people are frightened of spiders. But they help us, too. Spiders catch and eat mosquitoes, which bite us and can pass on disease. They also hunt flies, which carry germs that are harmful to people.

Ladybugs eat plant pests like greenflies and blackflies.

MINIHUNTERS

Even small spiders are hungry hunters. They help us by catching tiny insects such as gnats and midges, which may bite us.

Find Out for Yourself

More Books to Read

Burnie, David. *Inside Guides: Microlife*. New York, N.Y.: Dorling Kindersley Family Library, 1997.

Frankel, Alona. *Prudence's Get Well Book*. New York, N.Y.: HarperCollins, 2000.

Morris, Ann, and Ken Heyman. *Bread, Bread, Bread*. New York, N.Y.: HarperCollins, 1993.

Using the Internet

Explore the Internet to find out more about microlife that helps us. Use a search engine and type in a keyword such as bread, yeast, yogurt, or pollen, or the name of a particular type of microlife.

Glossary

antibiotics medicine that kills germs called bacteria

bacteria tiny living things. Some bacteria are helpful and some cause disease.

bio-vat large tank or container for growing microlife

diabetes condition where the body cannot use sugar to get energy, and may become very sick without treatment

fungi group of living things including mushrooms, toadstools, and yeasts, which cause rotting or decay

injection way of putting substances into the body using a sharp, hollow needle

microscope equipment to make very small things look bigger

moldy going bad or becoming rotten due to mold, a type of fungus

nectar sweet juice that is found inside certain flowers

nutrients substances used by living things to grow and stay healthy

penicillin medicine that kills many kinds of bacteria

pollen tiny, dustlike grains that pass between flowers, so they can make seeds

vaccine substance that prevents the body from catching a certain disease in the future

vegetarian person who eats mainly plant foods. Vegetarians do not eat foods made from animals.

yeast a type of tiny fungi

Index